London Philharmonic

To Paul & Betty
With all good wishes
from
Rex & Peggy.
1986.

London

MUSIC MAKERS SINCE 1932

Philharmonic

BY WILLIAM KALLAWAY

WITH AN INTRODUCTION

BY RICHARD BAKER

 KENNETH MASON

Published by Kenneth Mason, Homewell, Havant, Hampshire

Designed by Sadlergraphics and printed by Coasby Plus Ltd, Southsea, Hampshire

ISBN   0 900534 75 3

Contents

The title 'World Music Capital' has moved around many of the capitals of Europe during past centuries. It now rests upon London, home of the London Philharmonic and the pivot of its music activities. The attainment of this title has been realised only in recent years and it now sets the scene for this book about the London Philharmonic.

Under the heading 'London – Music Capital of the World' a number of people, well-known for their close interest and involvement in music, have kindly given some thought as to why this is so. To them and to the many who have contributed either by written word or interview, to those who have sought out treasured photographs, and to the Orchestra's management and staff at 53 Welbeck Street, London, I express my sincere thanks for their help.

Acknowledgement is made for the use of the following photographs: Radio Times, Hulton Library: pages 19, 23, 30 (Rubinstein's wife), 31, 33 (Queens Hall), 35, 36 (Sir Henry Wood), 38, 41, 47, 54 (Festival Hall), 90. LPO: 18, 20, 22, 24, 31 (Bravington & Casals), 42, 45. C. Busby: 61, 67 (Stage band, Glyndebourne), 82, 86 (Keith Whitmore), 88, 91 (2), 92, 93, 99, 100. G. Macdominic: 5 (Paul Tortelier). 94, EMI Records: 26, 27, 28, 29, 31 (Solomon), 33 (Joan Hammond), 46, 73, 94. Frew Frances Publicity Services: 26 (Sir Robert Mayer). Keystone: 30 (Artur Rubinstein). Bernard & Kruks: 32 (Tom Russell). Houston Rogers: 48. The Sunday Times: 50. Fox Photos: 54 (Festival Hall). Decca: 87. Allegro Studios: 58. F Bass, Allegro: 120. Evening Standard: 59. Hurok attractions, New York: 62 (W. Steinberg). Associated Newspapers: 62 (Vaughan Williams). W. G. Atkins: 64 (Boarding plane). Illustrated London News: 69. Guy Gravett: 70. F. Woods: 75, 76 (2). R. Coleman of Baron Studios: 77. BBC: 86 (Paul Beard). Clive Barda: 95. H. Breslin, New York: 98.

London - music capital of the world

❝London is more than fortunate in its orchestras. Nowhere else can one find such a diversity, not only of talent, but also of traditions. This wealth gives us unparalleled opportunities to hear all the world's great music. The London Philharmonic Orchestra has its unique part to play in this diversity and I am very pleased to send it my greetings on its fortieth anniversary❞

EDWARD HEATH 1972

❝The contribution of the London Philharmonic Orchestra to the growing reputation of London as a world centre for music needs no recommendation from me. We are indeed fortunate in having the services of four major symphony orchestras as well as a great volume of other musical activity, both in London and the provinces. All this activity is the result of a joint enterprise: by the public, the local authorities, as well as the state. The joint support is good for independence and I sincerely hope that it will continue to grow so that music can flourish❞

LORD ECCLES 1972

❝London is no longer the capital city of the great Empire, but we can take pride in what it has to offer in the world of the arts in general and music in particular. I am very proud that during the years when I had responsibility for the Arts we were able to promote some of our great arts endeavours, and at the same time make much better financial provision for our orchestras, great and small, in London and throughout the country. Too many people are inclined to forget that artists, like the rest of us, have got to live. All too often we are inclined to take unfair advantage of their talent and their dedication❞

JENNIE LEE 1972

❝I have always been proud to have participated in the foundation of the London Philharmonic Orchestra and also to have witnessed the growth of the Orchestra due to the devotion of Thomas Russell and later and since to Eric Bravington. The prominent position of London in the world of music is universally acknowledged; the London Philharmonic Orchestra can rightly claim to have actively contributed to this remarkable achievement❞

SIR ROBERT MAYER 1972

The London Philharmonic Orchestra is "primus inter pares" among London's other three first class symphony orchestras which, with the BBC orchestras, the orchestras of Covent Garden and now at the Coliseum for Sadlers Wells, contribute most substantially towards making London the leading musical capital of the world. It is capable of performances as good as those achieved by any of the great Continental orchestras and on the right occasion, with the right conductor and the right music, it scales the heights. When the Barbican Hall is completed, we shall have in London a sufficiency of halls to justify the quality and number of the orchestras. Almost every night of the week in almost every week of the year, London offers a range of music that caters for every conceivable musical taste. Two permanent opera companies, two large-scale ballet companies, other smaller-scale ballet companies of a less formal and more experimental character, chamber orchestras, recitals, the old Wigmore Hall night after night voluntarily introducing the new musical aspirants, concerts as far afield as Croydon and Swiss Cottage—support London's claims to give as good and better than most capital cities. With programmes ranging from the time-honoured classic to the newest of musical forms, no one goes unsatisfied. If we have declined as a great imperial power and wobble slightly in our industrial attainments, we can proudly claim that our musical culture, in terms of what can be furnished to the public, is as good and better than we have ever known. And with Britten, Walton, Tippett, Williamson, Bennett and others, we have a tally of composers worthy of our performing musicians

LORD GOODMAN 1972

The growth of musical talent, the availability of music everywhere and the relaxing attitudes towards the formality of music have contributed to London being acclaimed as the music capital of the world. The London Philharmonic has, where possible, encouraged these trends and enjoys its position at the forefront of London's musical life

SIR ADRIAN BOULT 1972

8

A miracle of
fire and beauty

INTRODUCTION BY RICHARD BAKER

In recent years, my work on BBC radio and television has brought me into contact with many of the leading orchestras of the world: the London Philharmonic ranks high among them, and I feel honoured to introduce these impressions of the life of the LPO in its fortieth birthday year.

But how to begin?

Perhaps simply by recalling what the London Philharmonic has meant to me personally over the years—an enthusiastic concert-goer and music lover who, through a happy professional chance, has been able to work with the great ones of the musical world.

The other day I was going through my old '78' gramophone records, trying to decide (as I've so often tried before) whether to get rid of them—after all, they take up a lot of space and rarely get played these days. Out came a pile of Columbia blue labels and HMV Red and Plum labels—they included works like the Swan Lake Ballet Music, conducted by John Barbirolli, Mozart's G Minor Symphony under Kussevitsky, the same composer's Sinfonia Concertante with Albert Sammons and Lionel Tertis as soloists and Sir Hamilton Harty conducting, Kreisler playing the Mendelssohn Violin Concerto and Weingartner directing Beethoven's Fourth Symphony. All these records, which I bought as a schoolboy in the late thirties and early forties, had one thing in common—the orchestra in each case was the London Philharmonic, recorded in their first blaze of brilliance during the years just before the Second World War. Needless to say, back went my old records into their case—reminders of my first encounters with fine music, and far too evocative to be thrown away.

Through records, then, I was already familiar with the splendours of the London Philharmonic Orchestra, when I read in the *Northampton Chronicle and Echo* that the Orchestra was to appear at the New Theatre there one day in the early 1940's. I had been evacuated to that town from London when the war broke out, and my music-loving friends and I were for ever lamenting (with precocious snobbery) the lack of good music in 'the provinces'. Well, here it was, on our doorstep, and what a thrill that concert gave us all. A thrill Northampton shared, as I now know, with innumerable towns and cities all over the country; for, during its second great period, the London Philharmonic Orchestra, labouring under untold difficulties, managed to keep symphonic music alive in Britain in the grimmest days of the war.

Twenty years later—in the mid-sixties, I heard an electrifying performance by the London Philharmonic of Mozart's Haffner Symphony. The Orchestra's President, Sir Adrian Boult, was conducting an astonishingly young body of players—and what thrust and energy that 'new look' Philharmonic of the sixties had! I remember meeting a string player after that Haffner performance and asking how it was that Sir Adrian Boult achieved such dazzling results with so little apparent exertion on his part. 'Well,' said the player, 'this morning, Sir Adrian stopped the rehearsal and asked why we were not making more effort. A member of the orchestra explained it was because Sir Adrian, at this final rehearsal, was making only minimal gestures on the rostrum. "Oh," said Sir Adrian, "you've got it quite wrong. The idea is that *I* should do less and less, but *you* should do more and more!"' At the concert it was clear the orchestra had got the message. And just one more characteristic glimpse of the London Philharmonic at work at one of its regular concerts in the Royal Festival Hall, with Bernard Haitink conducting Schubert's Great C major Symphony. What a superlative instrument the orchestra is now, under the man who has been the London Philharmonic's Principal Conductor and Artistic Director since 1967—an instrument of infinite flexibility, capable of responding to every shade of interpretation from the smoothest and most sensitive pianissimo to onslaughts of power which take the mind by storm.

Four personal encounters with the London Philharmonic, taken from four episodes of its existence: like me, every other music lover in Britain will have his or her own special memories of the LPO. But of course we can't leave it like that. We must try to look more objectively at the orchestra's history—to create a frame for the words and pictures which follow in these pages.

Beecham's boys

In 1931, Beecham discussed the possibility of a new orchestra with Robert Mayer who was associated with the Royal Philharmonic Society, the Courtauld Sargent Concerts and the Royal Choral Society, as well as running his own Children's Concerts. Through Mayer, Beecham secured the promise of engagements from all these organisations, and when the millionaire Samuel Courtauld put up £30,000, the dream orchestra took a substantial step towards reality: a board was formed consisting of Courtauld and Mayer with Beecham as Artistic Director. Protracted discussions and negotiations went on behind the scenes for a year; then, suddenly, while they were appearing at the Three Choirs Festival in September 1932, some two dozen fine orchestra players were astonished to receive telegrams inviting them to join Beecham in a totally new orchestra. Loyalty, for the most part, proved unequal to such an invitation and, within a fortnight, the London Philharmonic Orchestra had come into being, 106 strong. In all, Tommy was able to offer a guarantee of some 70–80 concerts annually, plus the International Opera Season at Covent Garden: it was an irresistible package, on which the glamour of Beecham's name set the seal.

There were no less than thirteen rehearsals—six of them for full orchestra—before Beecham was ready to bring his new creation before the public. The legendary debut of the London Philharmonic Orchestra took place on October 7, 1932, in the old Queen's Hall in Langham Place. The auditorium was only three quarters full, but Tommy was undeterred. 'Come on, Paul' he said to his leader, Paul Beard, just before stepping onto the platform, 'Let's show 'em what we can do!' The effect of the very first notes was electrifying. When it was all over the critics were of one mind: London, they agreed, had never in all its history heard an orchestra like this.

It was the start of the London Philharmonic's first triumphant period. In the six years before the outbreak of World War Two, this 'orchestra of virtuosi', under the sparkling leadership of Sir Thomas Beecham, easily dominated the musical scene in London—and beyond.

There were visits abroad—to the Brussels exhibition of 1935, when the music parts got lost before the Orchestra's crucial first-ever appearance on the Continent, and the concert began an hour late, after a frantic search through the library of the local Philharmonic Society had produced some tattered parts of various familiar items—only one of which, Mozart's G Minor Symphony, had been in the planned programme! Nevertheless the Orchestra won rave notices, as it did in Paris in March 1937. But surely the most extraordinary foreign visit was that in 1936 to Nazi Germany. Hitler himself presided at the first concert in Berlin's Philharmonic Hall, his appearance greeted by Nazi salutes—and the sotto-voce comment to the Orchestra's leader from Sir Thomas: 'It's bloody hot in here, I wish the place would go up in flames!' At the official reception afterwards, Beecham stood on a table to conduct 'Ach du lieber Augustin' and 'The More We are Together'—and only twelve members of the LPO managed to stagger along to rehearsal next day! After Berlin, the extensive tour took in, among many other places, Leipzig—where the statue of Mendelssohn had just been removed from the Gewandhaus—and Munich, where all Jewish members of the city's orchestra had been dismissed: sinister portents of what was to come. But the members of the London Philharmonic enjoyed themselves for the most part—one of their number remarking at a party that 'touring would be very pleasant, if it were not for the concerts!'

High among the achievements of the LPO in the thirties must rank their work in the orchestra pit at Covent Garden during the International opera seasons. Here Sir Thomas Beecham ruled supreme over all the great operatic stars of the day—names like Lotte Lehmann, Tiana Lemnitz, Frieda Leider, Lauritz Melchior, and Elisabeth Schumann; and to demonstrate the public's gullible adoration of foreigners, Beecham created another 'foreign celebrity' of his own when he passed off the established English soprano Dora Labbette as 'the new Italian nightingale, Lisa Perli'.

Ecstatic notices about the Orchestra's playing at this time abound, but Beecham drove them almost beyond endurance with rehearsals that began at ten a.m. and stretched on almost till curtain-up; then, just when mutiny threatened, he would stop everything and send his valet over to the Nag's Head for champagne and stout all round— and one night he took the third act of Siegfried at almost double speed because, as he explained, 'the public houses would close at 11—my orchestra had been slaving away since six o'clock and were thirsty—so I just let Wagner rip!' Few musicians could resist the exasperating charm of the man, and there was probably truth in the critical opinion that the LPO were 'never at their best when Beecham was not on the rostrum': for Tommy, as Neville Cardus put it in the *Manchester Guardian*, somehow contrived 'to make instrumentalists play miles above their normal selves'.

Difficulties were ahead, however. London apparently could not support even one orchestra, even in those days, in the style it deserved. More and more fell on Beecham's shoulders alone; two influential backers resigned from the non-profit making company that ran the orchestra, and there was an unsuccessful appeal for £20,000 to give it an assured future. Somehow Beecham, pouring out his own money as had so often happened in his early days, managed to put on the 1939 opera season, conducting sixteen of the thirty-five performances himself. But that, it seemed, was that. Afterwards his doctors told him imperatively that he must rest for a year; and with war becoming daily more inevitable in that summer of 1939, no one else was prepared to find money for the London Philharmonic.

Music at War

Totally uncertain of the future, but determined to make the most of the last few weeks of peace, the players went off on holiday, and got back to find a liquidation meeting called at the Holborn Restaurant for September 18. Briefly and bluntly Beecham told the creditors that there was nothing for anyone; when they had left, he turned to the members of the Orchestra and placed the future firmly in their hands. They were determined to carry on somehow. A proposal was made to put the whole orchestra in uniform for the duration of the war, but the Government were not interested. Then, after a series of hectic meetings in teashops and pubs, a company called Musical Culture Ltd was formed and on October 1, 1939 only a fortnight after it had been liquidated, the Orchestra resurrected a plan to visit Wales and came to life again in Cardiff, having managed to borrow £97 for the rail fares from a wealthy industrialist with his eye on the conductor's baton.

From now on the London Philharmonic was to do most of its wartime work far from London, bringing music to many a town which had never before had a visit from a symphony orchestra, and discovering, in those dark days and darker nights, a profound hunger for music among ordinary people who would never have dreamed of going to the Queen's Hall or Covent Garden in the old days, even if they could have afforded it.

But early 1940, saw a brief afterglow of the Orchestra's pre-war international grandeur. Some months were spent stockpiling recordings with Beecham for later release and giving concerts with the great man—including a notable one at the Queen's Hall in aid of the Finns, then desperately hard-pressed by the invading Russians.

After that, Sir Thomas decided to depart from these shores for three years—to Australia first and subsequently to Canada and the United States. This was a great blow to the Orchestra—a projected tour to South Africa had to be cancelled on the grounds that without Sir Thomas it would be Hamlet without the Prince. And more disappointments were to come. The Orchestra was due to play a prominent part in a festival to consolidate the Anglo-French alliance: on the day of the first concert France capitulated. Then there was a plan for a three-day festival on the south coast: on the opening evening Brighton had its first air raid, and the audience stayed at home. Once again, it seemed the Orchestra must die.

But in that dark summer of 1940, the London Philharmonic, like Britain as a whole, driven back on lonely defiance through the beaches of Dunkirk, was utterly determined not to be beaten. The Orchestra, led by a resourceful committee, decided to make a bold appeal to the British people for their help. That committee invoked the aid of J. B. Priestley—himself, as someone called him, 'the common man raised to the nth degree', and the most popular broadcaster in Britain after Churchill. Priestley laid the orchestra's plight before the public at a 'Musical Manifesto' at the Queen's Hall on July 18, 1940. The hall was packed. People were beginning to realise what would be lost if this great Orchestra perished; and a man who knew very well what the public wanted came to the rescue—dance band leader Jack Hylton.

For the next three years, theatres and music halls all over the country resounded to the unfamiliar strains of Beethoven, Mozart and Tchaikovsky—with the odd 'Rhapsody in Blue' and 'Warsaw Concerto' thrown in to leaven the diet. Right through the blitz the work went on, and no concert was cancelled. The LPO appeared in Coventry the day after one of the worst raids there. Travelling was a nightmare. Often the musicians had to bed down in freezing station waiting rooms, or in the hall where they had just played.

The wartime policy was well-conceived: by 1943 the LPO, engaged on a contract basis and with full pension provisions, had become the first full-time permanent Symphony orchestra to balance its budget without subsidy. And for a brief time, at the Orpheum Cinema, Golders Green, it had come near to realising the dream of every orchestra—a home of its own, where music was to be the main-spring of a wide-ranging centre for the arts.

Problems and progress

The architect of the Orchestra's fortunes at this time, indeed until 1952, was the man elected managing director and chairman by his fellow-musicians—the former viola player Thomas Russell. Required reading for anyone interested in the first ten tempestuous years of the LPO are his two excellent books, *Philharmonic* and *Philharmonic Decade*. A dedicated socialist, he made the London Philharmonic Orchestra into a self-governing co-operative, and campaigned throughout his musical career for democracy in music. But this did not prevent him from feeling, at the end of the war, that the Orchestra would never fully be itself until Sir Thomas Beecham returned.

However, a man of Beecham's temperament could not accommodate the idea of being engaged by an orchestra as Principal Conductor: it was he who had to engage them! And so in 1946, he broke away and formed the Royal Philharmonic. As Walter Legge of EMI had created the Philharmonia the year before, the long-established London Philharmonic and London Sympony Orchestras had to survive yet more poaching of good players. But for all that, the immediate post-war years were good ones for the LPO.

At their invitation, great conductors like Bruno Walter, Furtwängler, de Sabata, Kussevitsky, Kleiber, Ansermet and Münch were brought back to the London scene, and promising new-comers such as Georg Solti, Erich Leinsdorf, Leonard Bernstein, Sergu Celibidache and Jean Martinon were introduced to the British public. These were years distinguished by the performance and recording of much modern British music—a useful, but perhaps not popular policy for, in the mid-fifties, the LPO again found itself insolvent, and forced to abandon contracts and pension arrangements in favour of the fee-earning system which has prevailed in London ever since. In those bad times, the Orchestra was even driven to splitting the personnel and touring two Mozart orchestras simultaneously!

From that low point, the fortunes of the LPO have steadily improved. In the early 1960's, the Orchestra was drastically re-shaped—perhaps even revolutionised. It was then that one began to notice the large number of young players on the platform. This infiltration of new talent has blossomed brilliantly since 1967—when Bernard Haitink became Principal Conductor and Artistic Adviser. It is fitting that John Pritchard, too, should reap the benefit of his own foundation-laying: he does so every time the Orchestra appears in the pit of the Glyndebourne Opera House, where they have been resident since 1964, and where John Pritchard is Musical Director.

In the years since 1956 when they became the first-ever British orchestra to visit the Soviet Union, the London Philharmonic have collected golden opinions all around the world, on tours which have taken them to the Far East and Australia, to the United States, Mexico and Canada, as well as to all the principal centres of Europe: you will find many of the LPO's post-war triumphs recalled in this book. Nor must we forget to mention the Orchestra's partner over the last twenty-five years in many of its most memorable concerts and recordings—the London Philharmonic Choir. You will find more about the Choir later in these pages, let us just say here that it became the pioneer of London's orchestral choirs when it was adopted by the London Philharmonic Orchestra in 1947: that it had a most distinguished 22 years under the guidance of the late Frederic Jackson; and that John Alldis is now leading it into advanced areas of music where no other large British chorus has yet ventured.

Forty—and the future

And so, in 1972, the London Philharmonic Orchestra reaches its fortieth birthday. No great age, the older ones among us like to feel, though when we look back on the crises the Orchestra has been through, it seems astonishing it has survived that far. But the effect perhaps has been, paraphrasing Othello, to make the public love the LPO 'for the dangers it has passed'—as well as for the superb music-making it gives us today.

Any birthday of course, is a time for looking forward as well as back. The approach to the London Philharmonic's fortieth birthday year sees it at the peak of its powers, with an astonishing average attendance of over 90 per cent at its Festival Hall concerts. And yet the future seems no less problematic than the past. Eric Bravington, one-time Principal Trumpet of the LPO and the orchestra's managing director since 1959, with his small permanent staff are still much preoccupied with financial problems, at a time when it costs around half a million pounds a year to run a major orchestra, and when the LPO's portion of public grants to the London orchestras amounts to no more than 17% of the budget. Sharing a conductor, as they do, with the Concertgebouw Orchestra of Amsterdam, they are sharply aware of the different state of affairs in Europe where their Dutch colleagues, to take one example, are subsidised to the extent of no less than 85 per cent of their expenditure. There is no sign at present that the London Philharmonic, after the age of forty, will be able to let up on an over-taxing round of concerts, opera, recordings and tours. And however hard they work, when the players individually reach the age of sixty, there is as yet no pension to look forward to. That is a matter which very much concerns the London Philharmonic Orchestra Council, formed in 1965 and now working under the chairmanship of the Earl of Shaftesbury. Let us hope that before many more birthdays have gone by, the members of the London Philharmonic Orchestra, like their counterparts in Europe, will be able to enjoy more reliable rewards than they do at present for a lifetime of skilful and devoted work.

Though there are problems in plenty in the background, forty years of the London Philharmonic really is something to celebrate—and we hope this book will help to mark the occasion. In it you will find any number of tributes to the Orchestra from the great, and from it I hope you will gather the feel of a great orchestra's life.

So, a Happy Birthday, LPO!—and may you continue to delight us, as you did in the Queen's Hall at that very first concert on October 7, 1932, with playing which is— to quote Ernest Newman's words—'a miracle of fire and beauty'.

❛ . . . The LPO continues to lead in London's orchestral Grand National, both by the quality of its playing and the size of its audiences. ❜

❛ . . . The virtuosity displayed in the "Fantastique" left little doubt that, after forty years, the LPO is again the white-haired boy of London's concert audiences ❜

SUNDAY TIMES, APRIL 1972—CRITICISM ENTITLED
THE SOLTI TOUCH BY FELIX APRAHAMIAN

THE ROYAL PHILHARMONIC SOCIETY

INSTITUTED 1813

Patrons—THEIR MAJESTIES THE KING AND QUEEN

1932—1933

ONE HUNDRED AND TWENTY-FIRST SEASON

QUEEN'S HALL

SOLE LESSEES   MESSRS. CHAPPELL & CO., LTD.

FIRST CONCERT

Friday, October 7th, 1932, at 8.15 p.m.

Overture: "Le Carnaval Romain" - - -	Berlioz
Symphony No. 38, in D ("Prague") - - -	Mozart
An English Rhapsody: "Brigg Fair" - -	Delius

INTERVAL

Symphonic Poem: "Ein Heldenleben" - - -	Strauss

Conductor - - - SIR THOMAS BEECHAM

FIRST PUBLIC APPEARANCE
OF

THE LONDON PHILHARMONIC ORCHEST

Sir Thomas Beecham benefactor of music

1

The London Philharmonic Orchestra was the inspiration of Sir Thomas Beecham, so it is fitting that this book, published in the fortieth year of the Orchestra's life, should begin with a tribute to the man whom the *Times* on March 9, 1961 described as 'conductor-impresario, benefactor of music'. To enlarge this tribute by adding wit, raconteur and probably the greatest character of British music would not be unreasonable; for the great memorials to Sir Thomas are the orchestras which he founded and the anecdotes about him which are legend. Sir Thomas was born in 1879 in St Helens to a wealthy manufacturer of pills. Throughout his life he was steeped in music, founding amateur and professional orchestras, touring, conducting and generally involving himself with the vitality and enthusiasm for which he was so noted in every corner of British music. His memory was prodigious for he conducted everything except concertos and operas without a score. He rehearsed, according to some orchestral players, in' broad outline, defining very little but relying upon his enormous personality to produce the very best results'. Every musician in the orchestra which he formed was hand picked; they were in fact moulded to his style, almost as an extension of his own personality.

To quote the *Times*, 'in speech he was often indiscreet and took pleasure in indiscretion. He allowed his wit unrestrained play.' His witticisms were always to illustrate a point, but they were often discouraging to his musicians, particularly the younger ones. On being questioned about the future of young conductors during a television interview, Sir Thomas replied, 'why is it that English orchestras will engage so many third-rate conductors from abroad when we have so many second-rate ones of our own'. His extravagances too were noted: for instance he walked through the London streets one early spring wearing a fur coat. As the morning progressed it became warmer and Sir Thomas removed his coat, hailed a passing cab, threw the coat into the back seat and said, 'follow me around my man'.

A music debunker, dilettante, cavalier of music and brilliant musician, Sir Thomas was not universally popular. The suggestion that there are too many orchestras in London can be squarely laid at his door, an opinion echoed by Sir Adrian Boult's comment, 'Sir Thomas, expedient like Lloyd George, formed orchestras for the whim of the moment'.

C

Nevertheless the first concert of the London Philharmonic Orchestra on October 7, 1932, was greeted with press acclaim:

'The London Philharmonic Orchestra's explosive and brilliant inaugural under Beecham (it began with a Carnaval Romain overture which had people standing—some of them on their seats—to cheer) happened on October 7, 1932 . . .'

'In the course of nine minutes, the standards of British orchestral playing were raised to a level never before attained'.

One man who was closely involved with Sir Thomas during those early days was John

● Sir Thomas Beecham, left and right, at early rehearsals of his newly-founded orchestra, each man hand-picked. 'Once', said Alan McDougall, an LPO viola player, 'conducting a particularly fiery passage, Sir Thomas jabbed his baton through his hand. Pausing a moment, he picked off each protruding half, continued and, after the rehearsal had finished, went to hospital to have the lodged part removed.'

Denison, then a principal horn with the Orchestra, and now the Director of the Royal Festival Hall complex. He recalled two particular occasions which revealed certain aspects of the man's character.

'During a London Philharmonic provincial tour in the mid-thirties, we arrived rather late in the afternoon to give a concert at Swansea. It was Sir Thomas's first visit to the Brangwyn Hall, then pretty new. Since the programme was identical to that of concerts on preceding dates, there was no rehearsal, and Sir Thomas first saw the interior, with its famous and striking murals, while making his entry on to the platform as the concert began. Bowing deeply and slowly he took his time in looking around and acknowledging the thunderous applause. Then turning round to face the Orchestra, but before raising his baton, he addressed one of the players sitting immediately in front of him, and the following dialogue ensued in a penetrating sotto voce which all could hear:

'A remarkable building, Mr . . .'

'Yes, Sir Thomas, but it would be better if there was a bar in it.'

'You surprise me, Mr . . .; if my nostrils do not deceive me, I should certainly have thought that there was one close at hand. What is the overture?'

'A post-war story from my days at the Arts Council, which happened during a meeting in Sir Thomas's flat to discuss the raising of guarantees to finance the production of a

● 'In the LPO's archives this photograph of the most infamous men of the century is now a valuable collector's item. It shows Hitler, Goebbels and von Blomberg listening to the LPO in the Berlin Opera House, 1936.

Delius opera. Sir Thomas was in his silk dressing gown, large cigar going well, and very relaxed. The production budget which had been under discussion was of daunting proportions, and he wished me to understand that this was mainly due to the necessity, nowadays, of paying great attention to the scenic and visual aspects of an operatic production.

'Many years ago when such things were regarded as of less importance, I was rash enough to stage a performance of *Tristan and Isolde* at, I think, King's Lynn. As was frequently done at that time, a note of our requirements was sent in advance to the local manager of the theatre telling him to provide these from his own stock of scenery. The importance of a tower in Act II had been stressed, where Brangaene could put the burning torch for the love scene, and position herself for the great 'warning' passage before the return of King Mark. There was no opportunity to rehearse in that theatre, and you can judge of my astonishment when the curtain rose upon Act II, and I saw none other than my old friend, the set for *Iolanthe* Act II with Big Ben in the background'.

Nazi Germany in the middle 1930's during its pursuit of cultural purity was anxious to establish a musical entente cordiale with Britain. Beecham and Furtwängler, who brought the Berlin Philharmonic to Britain, had discussed the possibility of a tour of Germany by the London Philharmonic several times.

Then when Sir Thomas was at the Royal Opera House, Covent Garden, immersed in the operatic season, a formal invitation to tour Germany arrived from von Ribbentrop, 'ambassador-at-large' of the German Reich. Despite some public opposition, it was

agreed to accept and the tour was planned for November, 1936 under the direction of Sir Thomas's German-Jewish general secretary, Dr Berta Geissmar, who had held a similar position with Furtwängler and the Berlin Philharmonic Orchestra until political Nazi blackmail had forced her to leave Germany some months earlier.

Just before the Orchestra left for Germany, a plan arrived which gave details of the arrangements made for their entertainment. Sir Thomas commented, 'I do not think this will do. If this entertainment guide is to be followed, I will have to get the Berlin Philharmonic Orchestra to play for me after the second concert of the tour'.

Advance publicity of the tour resulted in some twenty towns not included in the itinerary asking for a visit from the London Philharmonic. Unfortunately it was impossible to fit them in.

The programme itself was designed with infinite care. No Brahms or Beethoven because this would be 'carrying coals to Newcastle,' but some Mendelssohn was included.

● Rudolph Hess, in the front row, left, listens to the LPO at their concert in Munich, 1936.

Right, Donald Gilbert's bust of Sir Henry Wood

As soon as the Germans saw this, a missive arrived from an embarrassed von Ribbentrop requesting tactfully that it be withdrawn. 'No Jewish composers by order'. The Orchestra was given a tumultuous reception on its arrival and throughout the whole tour. In Dr Geissmar's book *The Baton and the Jackboot* there is a brief account of Sir Thomas's meeting with Hitler. After saying how glad he was that Sir Thomas had come to Germany with his Orchestra, Hitler said, 'I should have liked so much to come to London to participate in the Coronation festivities but I could not risk putting the English to the inconvenience which my visit might entail'. 'Not at all', replied Sir Thomas innocently, 'there would be no inconvenience. In England we leave everyone to do exactly as he likes'. The Führer was nonplussed.

Hitler and his entourage attended the first concert in Berlin on November 13, 1936. The programme was the Carnaval Romain, Haydn Symphony No 5, the Handel—Beecham suite, The Gods go-a-begging, and Elgar's Enigma Variations. Of the Carnaval Romain, John Denison remembers, 'it felt as though a vacuum had been created by the strength, and the precise finish of the brass at the end of the overture brought a gasp from the Berlin audience.'

It was during this concert that Sir Thomas, in a moment of intimacy with the Orchestra, said in an audible voice 'the old bloke (Hitler) seems to like it', forgetting that the concert was broadcast throughout Britain. His comments were ascribed by the BBC to a mystery voice.

On another occasion, following a concert, the Führer's Deputy, Hess, invited Sir Thomas to his house. Hess tried to ingratiate himself with Sir Thomas by declaring how he admired the discipline of the Orchestra, a quality he had not expected to find in a group of Englishmen. 'Well', replied Sir Thomas loftily, 'we English have our own brand of discipline, but it is not always recognised or comprehended elsewhere—for instead of accepting it from others, we impose it on ourselves.'

● **Our own brand of discipline we impose on ourselves, Sir Thomas told the Germans**

A flying start
- and the war years

2

One who helped to establish the LPO was Robert (later Sir Robert) Mayer, better known perhaps for his Children's Concerts (fifty years old in the 1972–3 season). He and Beecham first met in 1931 when they combined forces to save from disaster a tour of Great Britain by the Berlin Philharmonic under Furtwängler. After this initial joint enterprise Sir Thomas sought Mayer's co-operation to form a new orchestra, partly as a counterblast to the BBC with whom Beecham at that time found it hard to work harmoniously. The orchestra was created; arranging a programme was another matter. But Mayer's intimate connections with London's musical life enabled him to arrange for the orchestra to play for the Courtauld-Sargent Concert series and the Royal Philharmonic Society, of whose board Sir Robert was a member. They also played for the Royal Choral Society and at the children's concerts themselves.

With this sort of schedule, 60 per cent of the Orchestra's financial requirements were underwritten and the newly named London Philharmonic Orchestra was thus enabled to make a flying start. 'The board consisted of Samuel Courtauld and myself', said Sir Robert, 'and Lord Esher and Frederick d'Erlanger who resigned after four weeks. We were responsible financially, Beecham artistically. But the initial esprit de corps was not to last long. Courtauld and I, following differences between us and Beecham, resigned in 1936.' So after a stable, well endowed start the Orchestra and Beecham found themselves very much on their own.

War between members of a board is one thing. A full scale international war is another. Then, to make things even worse, Sir Thomas Beecham decided to live in America. With no future or figurehead the prospects for the Orchestra were bleak. It lacked financial support and a decision was made to disband. But the players themselves disagreed and decided instead to continue in the form of a co-operative under a board of directors elected by themselves. The first managing director was a player, Thomas Russell, who held down the job and kept the Orchestra together until 1952. This system of management continues to this day and is followed by other London orchestras. Among the really great names of musical renown four stood out in the Orchestra's early years: Artur Rubinstein, Pablo Casals, Solomon and Yehudi Menuhin. From his Highgate home Yehudi Menuhin reflected upon his association with the Orchestra.

● Sir Robert Mayer, above, and Lady Mayer, below, launched the first Children's Concert at the Central Hall, Westminster, during the bus strike of 1923.
Opposite, Yehudi Menuhin (left) one of Sir Henry Wood's 'children of music' with Bruno Walter (right)

'The London Philharmonic Orchestra and I are in one way contemporary, for our London history dates back to approximately the same period. In fact, I have a slight edge of two or three years. I can only say that rarely have four short decades been packed with so much activity and achievement. This great Orchestra has earned a unique place in the musical life of the most musical city in the world. Among its members are many of my favourite colleagues, and perhaps it is not beside the point to say the musicians and the staff together create one of the friendliest and most harmonious atmospheres I know.'

But in Beecham's day harmony was not quite so obvious. However, with Beecham in America, an unlikely partnership developed between dance band leader Jack Hylton and Dr Malcolm Sargent.

Hylton offered to arrange for the LPO, with Sargent as principal conductor, a fourteen-week tour of halls, cinemas, theatres and variety clubs in ten cities. Tom Russell immediately accepted, a decision he was certainly not to regret.

With Sargent, relieved on Fridays and Saturdays by Basil Cameron, the tour started in Glasgow, where 30,000 people attended. Two concerts a day was the minimum, with a third being fitted in at 1 pm if the others were at 3.30 pm and 5.45 pm. Fourteen concerts a week was the average. White tie and tail coat was the standard no matter the venue, and Dr Sargent continued to establish his reputation not only musically but sartorially as well—red carnation by day and white by night, despite the heaviest of air raids.

● Above, the young Menuhin with Toscanini. The picture on the left of Yehudi, already a world figure, was taken aboard ship in 1927. Right, just before a tour of Great Britain and his first appearance with the LPO, Yehudi, aged 15, is seated between Sir Edward Elgar (left) and Sir Thomas Beecham

ROYAL ALBERT HALL

Manager · · · · · · · · · CHARLES B. COCHRAN

Sunday, November 20th, 1932, at 3

HAROLD HOLT Announces
ONLY APPEARANCE THIS SEASON
YEHUDI MENUHIN
WITH THE
LONDON PHILHARMONIC ORCHESTRA

CONDUCTORS:
SIR EDWARD ELGAR
SIR THOMAS BEECHAM

PROGRAMME

Concerto No. 2 - Bach
in E major

Concerto No. 7 - Mozart
in D major

Concerto in B minor - Elgar

TICKETS, **3/6** TO **15/-**

●Left, Artur Rubinstein, pictured at his wedding in 1932, has been associated with the LPO from the days of Beecham. Below, at rehearsal for a concert with the LPO at the Festival Hall in December 1967. Right, top, Pablo Casals, then 86, conducted the LPO and the Choir in the 1963 British première of his oratorio, El Pessebre. Here seen receiving a presentation from Eric Bravington, the Orchestra's managing director

● Above, Pablo Casals as a young man.
Right, Solomon, whose appearances with
the Orchestra began in the early 1930s

Dr—later Sir Malcolm—Sargent's contact with the Orchestra had begun in 1932 and became particularly close from 1940 to 1967. So close, indeed, that the Orchestra look upon him as an honorary founder member. His last major appearance with the LPO was the 26,000 mile tour of 1962 (see pages 63 to 65). In the last five years of Sir Malcolm's life the Orchestra appeared under his direction in several of the Henry Wood Promenade Concerts.

No one who was there for the last night of the Proms on September 16, 1967, or who saw it on television will forget the unexpected entrance of Britain's best known conductor, the greatest of the Promenade gladiators, Sir Malcolm Sargent. It was Sir Malcolm's appearance which sent his 'beloved promenaders' into raptures of delight. Few knew the courage this appearance required or the finality of the gesture. Three weeks later Sir Malcolm, or 'Flash' as he was known to his younger followers, was dead and the Orchestra had lost a man who had contributed enormously to its beginnings.

But we are straying from chronology and the tenuous thread of our story. Concerts to packed houses in wartime London were common, with the Queen's Hall featuring more than most in London's music itinerary. The Orchestra played one such concert on a Saturday in 1941.

Leaving their instruments in a bandroom underground, in itself an unusual practice, the Orchestra's members left with the intention of returning the following morning

● Far left, Jack Hylton, the dance band leader who saved the Orchestra. Left, Thomas Russell, managing director of the LPO, 1940–1952. It was his pluckiness, said Sir Adrian Boult, that kept the Orchestra together in the war years. Above, the Queen's Hall, bombed in 1941. Right, Joan Hammond, whose singing cheered so many during the blitzes

● **Sir Malcolm Sargent conducting the LPO at Nottingham in a series presented twice daily in the theatres during the war**

to rehearse for a concert in the afternoon. But an air raid, retaliation perhaps for the destruction of the Berlin Opera House a few nights earlier, destroyed the Queen's Hall. The only part to survive included a small room above ground which contained those instruments too large for the bandroom underground! With those few remaining undamaged instruments and a hastily gathered motley of borrowed instruments the Orchestra still managed to honour its concert commitments that afternoon, but at the Duke's—not Queen's—Hall. Not a seat was empty; people queued on the pavements and hundreds were turned away. Three thousand letters offering replacement instruments resulted from a BBC appeal. People travelled across London clutching instruments, many of them cherished family heirlooms, to answer the appeal. After permission had been sought from the donors, some of those instruments which were not chosen

● Standing on the streamer-wreathed rostrum and wearing a garland of flowers presented by the Promenaders, Sir Malcolm Sargent receives the applause of the Albert Hall audience in 1952

for use were sent to the Red Cross for onward transmission to professional musicians who were prisoners of war.

On that particular episode Thomas Russell, writing in the *London Philharmonic Post* in 1941 commented: 'We have heard that there are a few people to whom the damage wrought on the Berlin Opera House offers some belated satisfaction for the loss we have undergone by the burning of our leading concert hall, but to us the double destruction is a single loss and on both sides music lovers must feel a sense of mutual deprivation.'

Whatever the devastation and whatever the difficulty of travelling the length and breadth of wartime Britain there were still many patriotic artists who undertook to tour with the Orchestra. One such, whose reputation is international, was Miss Joan

Hammond. From her diary of April 21 and 22, 1943, following two concerts with the Orchestra at Wolverhampton and Leicester, this extract is reprinted:
'Despite how weary the members of the Orchestra felt as a result of travel delays, food rationing and the accepted sleepless nights during raids, they played with amazing warmth and vitality which was very moving and a sheer joy to me, and to the audience.'
From her Australian home Miss Hammond recalled her vivid memories of the Orchestra in the 1940's.
'What a period of hopes, frustrations and cultural ebb and flow existed in the 1940–50 decade'. Orchestras suffered more than individual artists as so many of their players answered the urgent call to arms and left the orchestral ranks sadly depleted. But to the LPO this factor proved to be a perpetual challenge. The conditions under which they played were appalling but this orchestra gave an exemplary demonstration of unity and artistic achievement during the turmoil of World War II, that raised it from the musical chaos which existed.
'Conditions following the war were slow to improve but the LPO set about the gargantuan task of reforming its ranks and attaining first-rate recognition in Europe during the difficult post-war period. It would be true to say that the more it suffered the greater it became in the eyes and ears of its multitudinous supporters.
'I had the pleasure of a long and musically diversified association with this wonderful group of musicians and I always looked forward, with immeasurable pleasure, to "making music" with them.'

An artist's impression of the scene in a war-time aircraft factory during a performance by the Orchestra

The association with
Sir Henry Wood

3

Yet one more great name to add to those associated with the Orchestra at this period in its history is that of Sir Henry Wood. From the extract of Miss Hammond's wartime diary we move to one from Sir Henry's diary dated May 10, 1941, which reads:

'Easter Sunday was my last concert in the Queen's Hall, 'Parsifal'. The simplicity of this entry is an indication of his feeling towards the birth-place of his own Promenade Concerts. From the devastation of Queen's Hall was rescued the bust of Henry Wood which is still to be seen beneath the organ in the Royal Albert Hall during each Promenade season. His association with the London Philharmonic goes back to the middle 1930's, although there was an element of discord in his relationship with Sir Thomas Beecham. They were two entirely different characters, one relying upon personality, the other upon discipline to extract the finest orchestral performances. Sir Adrian

● **Sir Henry Wood rehearsing at the Queen's Hall in October, 1938. For him, to live was to make music**

●'And they do not know, and would not believe me if I told them, what the Promenade Concerts were like at Covent Garden in the eighteen-eighties. It was Wood who dragged British orchestral music alive out of that abyss.'
G. Bernard Shaw, New Year, 1944, in a tribute to Sir Henry Wood

Boult remembers congratulating Henry Wood upon the publication of *My Life in Music*. 'Yes', confided Wood, 'and there is no mention of Beecham, not even in the index'.

Henry Wood had a strong interest in musical education which found expression in his visits to Stowe School in 1938 with the Orchestra. He also watched over the careers of young soloists, his 'children of music'. One such, mentioned in Jessie Wood's *The Last Years of Henry J Wood*, is Yehudi Menuhin, who performed three violin concertos with the LPO in March 1938. Eight months later Henry Wood's jubilee was celebrated. Two hundred players, the combined strength of the London Philharmonic, BBC Symphony and London Symphony orchestras, gave a concert in the Royal Albert Hall with Rachmaninov as soloist. A second jubilee was that of his Promenade Concerts in 1944, the year of Sir Henry's death.

Sir Henry found the blackouts a time of intense misery relieved only by his music and an extensive programme of concerts. Throughout the war until his death, Sir Henry conducted the Orchestra principally during his Promenade series.

In the New Year of 1944 George Bernard Shaw wrote this tribute to Sir Henry remembering him and his services to music over a span of 50 years.

'And they do not know, and would not believe me if I told them, what the Promenade Concerts were like at Covent Garden in the eighteen-eighties. It was Wood who dragged British orchestral music alive out of that abyss. And after a life-work which would have staled and worn out anyone but Wood, when the wireless gave him an audience of millions to play to in the Albert Hall with a splendidly full band, he rose to the occasion and surpassed himself in performances which crowned him as a master of his art and peer of the greatest of his European rivals.'

Taking music to the people and making it live in the most unlikely venues, at the behest of the world's greatest conductors in this golden period, was the keystone of the creation of London as the music capital of the world.

From 1940 until 1948 the Orchestra was without a permanent Principal Conductor and Artistic Director although the responsibility was shared for some time between Anatole Fistoulari, Alceo Galliera and Jean Martinon. Beecham had returned to this country in 1945, presumably with the intention of taking over where he had left off five years earlier, but he did not like the terms of association offered and departed for new orchestral pastures. The rift, however, was not too wide, and he conducted many more Philharmonic concerts.

Taking up the baton in 1948 as Artistic Director and Principal Conductor was Eduard van Beinum, the first of two conductors in the Orchestra's life to hold concurrently a similar position with the Concertgebouw Orchestra, the second, of course, being Bernard Haitink. Van Beinum remained for three seasons with the Orchestra, the third season, because of heavy responsibility and poor health, being shared with Sir Adrian Boult.

During these years he performed the works of Mahler and Bruckner on many occasions,

● **Sir Henry was a craftsman in music and a craftsman in wood and metal as well**

often to almost empty houses. His perseverance at this early stage, however, is almost certainly the basis of the works' present fashionable popularity. An outstanding conductor, he became very much 'one of the boys'; which is not always to the best advantages of either a conductor or an orchestra. Yet despite any minor criticism in this direction which may have been forthcoming at the time, he conducted with a style of his own, giving many historic performances with Kathleen Ferrier, for whom he had a special affection.

Apart from adding considerably to the Orchestra's prestige, for the adulation of

Kathleen Ferrier's singing ability was world-wide, she will be remembered by so many for the warmth and charm of her personality.

In March, 1944 the Orchestra combined in a Henry Wood Memorial Concert with the BBC Symphony Orchestra and the London Symphony Orchestra directed by John Barbirolli, Sir Adrian Boult and Basil Cameron. The first musical post-war golden era for the London Philharmonic in particular and British music in general was from 1946–1950. Each year the Orchestra played at approximately 200 symphony concerts and were contracted 52 weeks of the year. The only other orchestra to rival such an achievement at this time was the BBC Symphony.

It was a glorious period of great names: Georg Szell, Clemens Krauss, Alceo Galliera, Erich Kleiber, Charles Münch, Ernest Ansermet, Jean Martinon, Erich Leinsdorf, Serge Koussevitzky, Carl Schuricht, Wilhelm Furtwängler, Bruno Walter, Eduard Van Beinum and Victor de Sabata. All came to London at the invitation of the London Philharmonic and other orchestras.

● **Edward Van Beinum (right), who was responsible for popularising the works of Mahler and Bruckner, with Sir Adrian Boult**

The London Philharmonic Choir

A lasting tribute to this period is the London Philharmonic Choir which is not tied exclusively to the LPO. It was born on May 15, 1947; on its anniversary 25 years later it was described as a 'virtuoso choir' by the *Daily Telegraph* following its performance of David Bedford's 'Star Clusters, Nebulae and Places in Devon', the first time the work had been heard. This had, in fact, been commissioned by the Orchestra. It was fitting tribute to the progressive approach by the Choir and Orchestra to contemporary music.

The Choir had started life, however, in a rather more staid fashion. Coached by their founder, Frederic Jackson, an acclaimed pianist and conductor, they performed Beethoven's Ninth Symphony, conducted by Victor de Sabata. It was a major triumph. For twenty-two years Jackson prepared the Choir for recordings and choral works under some of the world's most eminent conductors. Three months short of the Choir's twenty-fifth anniversary, Frederic Jackson died. Although he had handed over the responsibilities of his leadership in 1969 to John Alldis, his affection for the Choir remained until his death. The nucleus of the Choir in 1947 was a group of singers from Charles Kennedy Scott's Philharmonic Choir of the inter-war years. Their first recording was conducted by de Sabata.

During the preparation of this book many people have remembered affectionately their relationships with the Orchestra. In some cases it was necessary to talk with a friend or relation about this association. One of those was Mrs Eliana de Sabata Ceccato. 'My father had an immediate and wonderful relationship with the London Philharmonic and together they did many concerts. He always regretted not being able to stay permanently, as the LPO had offered him the position of principal conductor after his first rehearsal. He was very fond of this Orchestra and agreed to record with them, although recording to him was a nightmare. The result of one of the recordings was the widely acclaimed Beethoven's Third Symphony which regrettably is now unavailable. I hope that the London Philharmonic, with the dear memory of my father in their heart, continue their splendid way in the magic world of music'.

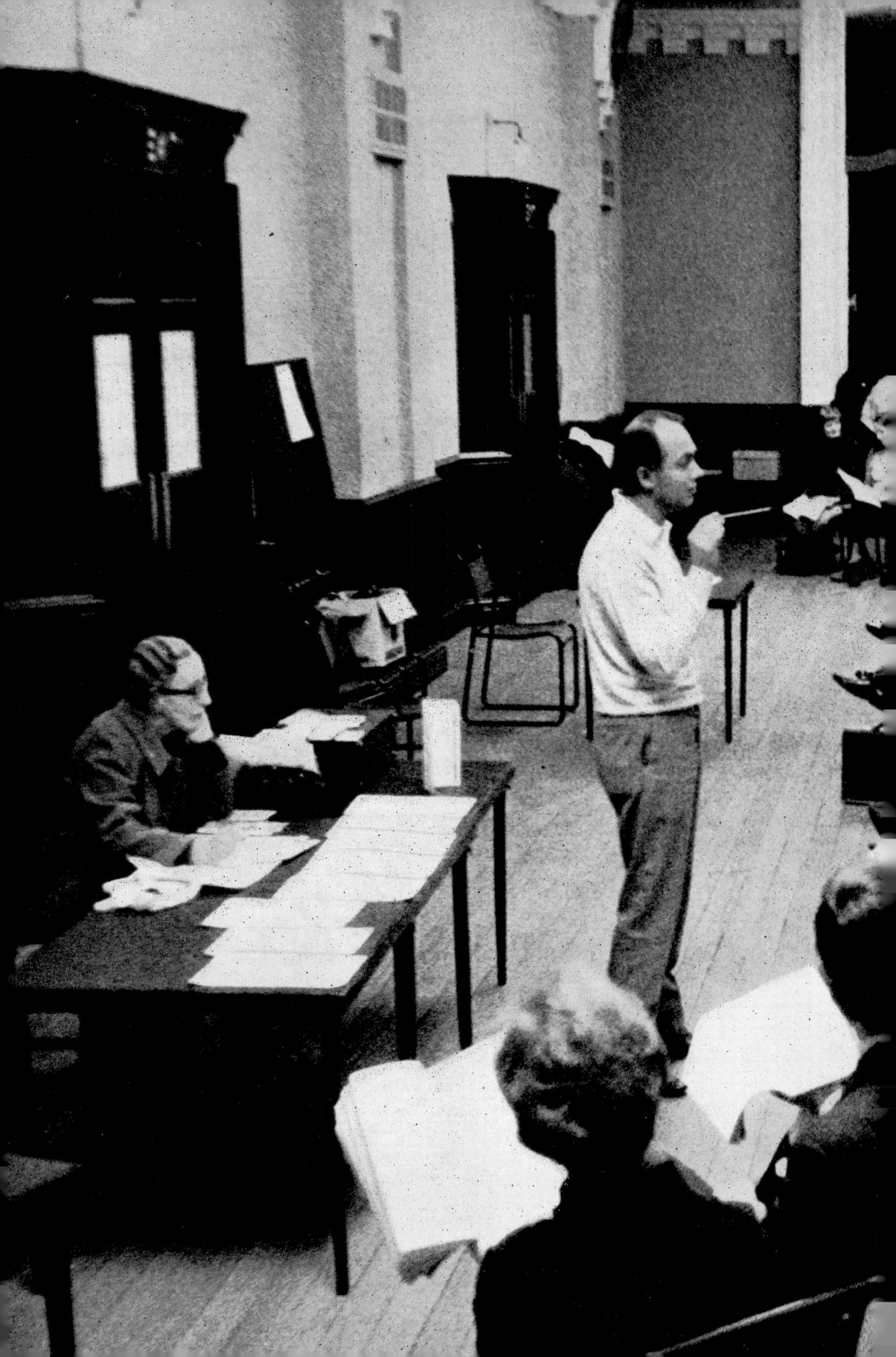

Above, 'Frederic Jackson was conductor of the London Philharmonic Choir for many years and brought that organisation to a high level of excellence,' wrote Dr Anthony Lewis in ''The Times''. The large picture shows John Alldis conducting a rehearsal of the London Philharmonic Choir

The recording was of Brahms's Alto Rhapsody with Kathleen Ferrier, the first of many memorable presentations which included, among others, the first London performance of Britten's Spring Symphony; the cathedral performances of Belshazzar's Feast at Ely, Gerontius for BBC television under Sir Adrian Boult at Canterbury, and performances at St Paul's and Westminster Abbey. Over the years the Choir have developed a particular affection for certain conductors. One such is Sir Adrian Boult from

● Above, Kathleen Ferrier walking with Peter Peers during the Edinburgh Festival, 1947. Left, Victor de Sabata who conducted the first recording of the London Philharmonic Choir

whom, according to Daniel Snowman, the Choir's chairman, the singers have gained an unrivalled knowledge of the choral works of Vaughan Williams, Holst and Elgar.

'There is a tremendous feeling of warmth and admiration, too, for Bernard Haitink with whom we have worked regularly since 1967. We also got off to a magnificent start with Sir Georg Solti in 1971 with a performance of Haydn's Creation. It was a truly exhilarating experience.'

Haitink was the conductor in 1972 when the critics with one voice called the Choir's performance of Britten's War Requiem one of the most inspired that the work had ever received.

Because the Choir is a non-professional organisation, its membership is in a constant state of flux. With two—sometimes more—rehearsals a week it means that the acclaimed music makers must devote a great deal of time to one of London's most respected choirs.

Although the Choir's memories of Sir Georg are recently acquired, his first association with an English orchestra was with the LPO a year after the Choir's formation, as he related in a recent conversation at the Royal Festival Hall —

'My first association with an English orchestra started in 1948 with a recording of

47

Left, Joan Sutherland.
Below, Sir Georg Solti
whose partnership with the
Choir is 'an exhilarating
experience' said Daniel
Snowman, Chairman of the
London Philharmonic Choir

Haydn's Drum Roll Symphony with the London Philharmonic. It was a decisive turning point in my life because, as a result, I made up my mind to stay in England and I am delighted to be able to say that my association with that Orchestra is closer than ever before and I recently signed an exclusive contract to work with them in London'.

Another person to make her debut with the Orchestra at this time was Miss Joan Sutherland. It was to be the first of many occasions over the years. Typical of the notices which followed these concerts is Stanley Sadie's in *The Times* in February 1969, the occasion, a London Philharmonic performance of Handel's 'Alcina'. 'Joan Sutherland, of course, produced some lovely, spacious, gleaming tone and some beautiful sustained line, also much brilliant fine detail . . .'

● **Above, Sir Georg Solti. Right, John Denison, one-time principal horn player with the Orchestra under Beecham**

The South Bank Sound

At the hub of London's music are the Royal Festival Hall, the Queen Elizabeth Hall and the Purcell Room, open for 364 days of the year. More than a million people a year attend functions there. John Denison, who was appointed General Manager at the Royal Festival Hall in 1965, is now the Director of that complex. Previously he was with the London Philharmonic in Beecham's time from 1933–1937.

The Orchestra played during the Festival of Britain in 1951, the year, of course, which saw the opening of the Royal Festival Hall. They also contributed to the series of eight concerts in 1953 to celebrate the coronation of Queen Elizabeth II in June.

Since then the Royal Festival Hall has been the main London concert venue of the LPO, the place in which it has built its reputation and where it has to be maintained in future years.

In the 1971–72 season, the London Philharmonic attracted to the Royal Festival Hall

● One of many tributes to Sir Adrian Boult. The Schwann Long Playing Catalogue Readers' Award presented for the recording of Vaughan Williams' Sea Symphony. Below, David Oistrakh introduces his son Igor to Sir Adrian during the Orchestra's 1956 tour of Russia

● Sir Adrian and the Orchestra in the Conservatoire, Moscow, in 1956
● Right, in the Great Hall of the Moscow Conservatoire, Sir Adrian and the boys from the Moscow Choir School who sang in Holst's 'Planets'

● Above, at the hub of London's musical life, the South Bank complex. Below, King George VI and Queen Elizabeth with Princess Elizabeth and the Duke of Edinburgh in the Royal Box on the opening night of the Royal Festival Hall on May 5, 1951

● The Coronation of James II taken from the programme of Eight Coronation Concerts, 1953. In the programme foreword Sir Arnold Bax, Master of the Queen's Musick, wrote, 'Music will play an honourable but naturally somewhat subsidiary part in the great ceremony on June 2, during which our young Queen will dedicate her life to the service of God and her country. The present series of concerts has been planned as a kind of adjunct to the Coronation, and in this less solemn atmosphere, we may fancy St Cecilia standing unattended before the throne, bringing as votive offering a "concourse of sweet sounds" to the further praise and glory of Her Majesty. God bless the Queen!'

2,855 paying people per concert, 94 per cent of capacity. This figure excludes the few complimentary seats and the reduced capacity brought about by choral concerts. John Denison attributed the reason for this outstanding success to the fact that the London public appreciated the sterling qualities of the partnership between the Orchestra and Bernard Haitink, their principal conductor.

In the Festival of Britain year Sir Adrian Boult became the Orchestra's principal conductor, a position which he retained until 1957.

Now its president, Sir Adrian began his association with the London Philharmonic in

the early war years. In his office high above one of London's musical landmarks, the Wigmore Hall, Sir Adrian reflected on those formative years:

'It was the pluckiness of Tom Russell that kept the Orchestra together in the war years. During this time Jack Hylton achieved much and Malcolm Sargent did some rather posh concerts, too. I was at the BBC during the critical period but we could do little to help. The LPO planned its programme only ten days in advance whereas we were working at least ten weeks ahead.

The BBC were so anxious to help the LPO that my services were given free of charge for a few days occasionally during the war. They were exhausting times.

● Many of the world's leading artists have played with the Orchestra. Above is Paul Tortelier; below, Isaac Stern and, left, Nathan Milstein

The Orchestra were most heroic—returning home, after slogging round the country, to bombed homes and bombed wives. They travelled the entire country, often for one night engagements, and where accommodation was unobtainable they sometimes had to resort to sleeping in station waiting rooms. I remember at Abingdon the entire Orchestra changed in a room which could have been no bigger than six by twenty-five feet.

'Then in 1950, at 61 years of age, according to the rule, I was sacked from the BBC and Tom Russell took me on the next day, For seven years I was a carpet-bagger, touring the country conducting almost every concert, sometimes for five or six performances a week.'

During a discussion, a brief part of which is included later, with Rodney Friend, the Orchestra's leader, he stated 'Sir Adrian represents all that is best about Britain and all that is best in British music.'

● Left, Sir Adrian Boult, President of the Orchestra. Below, Sir Adrian's 80th birthday. A presentation of this cake and a plaque from members of the Orchestra was made in April 1969 following a rehearsal at the Royal Albert Hall

There can be little doubt that this sentiment mirrors the feeling of the vast majority of musicians who have played under Sir Adrian. His constant association over the years with the Orchestra has contributed significantly to its present success.

During his years as Artistic Director many great artists began their association with the Orchestra, three of whom were Paul Tortelier, Isaac Stern and Nathan Milstein. Unfortunately space precludes giving many details of their concert performances or indeed their relationships with the Orchestra. To reflect however minimally upon these occasions, three press notices have been selected from the reams available, to act as nothing more than tokens of some memorable evenings.

'... Paul Tortelier, the cello soloist envisaging Don Quixote, was naturally at his most alluring in the romantic flights and phrases of his part; and his treatment of the "death scene," with the final slither, was as eloquent as well could be ...'

'... I recollect that it was the LPO, some 30 years ago, that directed by Sir Thomas Beecham, gave the finest performance ever of *Don Quixote*, an opinion shared by Strauss himself ...'

Neville Cardus, The Guardian

'... Mr. Stern's performance was as nearly perfect as I ever hope to hear it. Over the adagio, in particular, his finely spun yet diamond-firm tone cast an unbroken enchantment of an extraordinary nobility ...'

Martin Cooper, Daily Telegraph

'... It was a performance which recalled the young Milstein ... a violinist glorying in his technical mastery and the mellow sounds emanating from old sun-stained wood ...'

Neville Cardus, The Guardian

In 1956 just a few months before Sir Adrian resigned his position, the Orchestra broke entirely new ground in visiting the Soviet Union, the first British orchestra ever to do so. At this time, however, transport to the USSR presented problems. After flying to West Berlin, the players crossed into East Berlin by coach and there embarked upon a sixty-hour train journey through Poland to the Soviet Union. The constant reassurances by the Russian officials that refreshments would be provided for the journey resulted in a two-and-a-half-day sack of food thrust upon each member of the Orchestra just prior to departure from East Berlin.

Newspaper comments on their arrival in Moscow were less than gushing. They mirrored the political climate of the time, for the Orchestra left Britain on the day that a Russian athlete was suspected of shoplifting a hat in London, and things were distinctly cool on arrival.

If the newspaper was official the audiences for the ten-concert tour, six in Moscow and four in Leningrad, were not. Sir Adrian, the guest conductor and the Orchestra received a superb reception.

The critical
years

But despite all its international musical success, in 1957 the Orchestra faced bank-
ruptcy. The creditors, like so many operatic characters previously seen only from the
theatre pit, were at the door. So desperate was the position that all individual contracts were cancelled and the players accepted the penultimate step, before final
disbandment, of taking work on a single fee basis. Great sacrifices had to be made
by each of the players yet, despite the apparent bleakness of their situation, not one
deserted. They struggled on until early in 1959, when Eric Bravington, who had been
a trumpet player with the Orchestra since 1939, became managing director, a position
which he holds to this day.

For the next five years—until 1964—the crisis continued. Although there had been
no spare funds for improving artistic standards, the Orchestra from this point

● Eric Bravington has done a
prodigious job for the Orchestra.
A brilliant trumpeter during his
playing career, he is now the
most respected manager in
London, said Sir Adrian Boult
in 1972

concentrated on artistic matters and new young blood was brought in to form the basis of the Orchestra as it is today.

Sir Adrian Boult's name is always closely associated with the finest interpretation of the works of Dr Ralph Vaughan Williams, and in 1958 the Orchestra, with Sir Adrian, recorded eight of the nine symphonies for Decca. It was to be, that on the morning of Dr Vaughan Williams' death, the Orchestra were actually recording his Ninth Symphony.

There are many affectionate memories of this composer conducting. One in particular is remembered: 'During a rehearsal of Five Tudor Portraits for the 1934 Norwich Festival, Vaughan Williams stopped the performance, looked at his score and exclaimed, "nobody's playing what I've got!"'

The affection was mutual, as Ursula Vaughan Williams, his widow, recalls: 'his association with the London Philharmonic Orchestra was always a very happy one and it was they who played at his memorial service in Westminster Abbey on September 17, 1958. Sir Adrian conducted and their part of the service was a very generous and impressive contribution.'

Following the hectic years of the early and middle fifties under Sir Adrian, a period which did so much to increase the popularity and reputation of the Orchestra throughout Britain, one of Europe's top names took over the principal conductor's baton. For two seasons from 1958 to 1960 it was a time for development under Dr William Steinberg. With his tough discipline, humour and complete knowledge of what makes an orchestra tick, he began restyling the Orchestra's artistic approach. Apart from his training, Steinberg also successfully promoted contemporary English and American music which has since played a significant part in the Orchestra's artistic policy.

● **Below left, Dr William Steinberg, one of Europe's foremost orchestral trainers and a tough disciplinarian. Below right, Ralph Vaughan Williams during a rehearsal, shown here with Sir John Barbirolli**

● **At the Orchestra's 21st birthday. Sir Arthur Bliss, Dr Ralph Vaughan Williams and Sir Adrian Boult**

Although constant travelling between London and America became too much for Dr Steinberg and he reluctantly retired, his interest in the Orchestra he helped to develop remains to this day.

It was in the early 1960's that the Orchestra resolved to undertake world tours whenever the opportunity presented itself. The first of these, probably a result of their highly successful visit six years previously to Russia, was to be a world beater.

'London audiences shout their heads off for a full five minutes' was the indirect advice given to Hong Kong audiences at the end of a delighted columnist's piece in the China Mail one day early in 1962 when the news was given that the Orchestra intended to visit the island.

Checking the day of the week to establish which country you were in was just a fact of life during the Orchestra's mammoth 26,000-mile tour of 1962 which included 32 concerts in India, Hong Kong, the Philippines, Australia and Ceylon—the longest tour ever undertaken by a British symphony orchestra. Directed by Sir Malcolm Sargent and assisted by John Pritchard, who joined the tour in Australia, the Orchestra was acclaimed throughout.

To record all the ecstatic notices which the Orchestra has received on this tour would be repetitive. But this notice from the Calcutta Statesman of March 3, 1962 is typical: 'Sir Malcolm and the Orchestra were greeted with a prolonged, wildly enthusiastic and fully justified ovation.'

To be a focal point of the music capital is to be judged by international standards. To be parochial and stay within the confines of your own recognised home is easy—

63

● Top left, when the Orchestra boarded the plane Sir Malcolm Sargent read them a Godspeed telegram from the Queen.
Below left, Sir Malcolm is garlanded after the first concert in India.
Above, with Pandit Nehru. Below, with Henry Datyner, the Orchestra leader

but to measure standards it is important to tour, 'not only to assess other levels, but to promote and maintain your own reputation,' explains Keith Whitmore, chairman of the LPO.

It was in September 1962 that John Pritchard became the Orchestra's principal conductor. The following season he accepted the post of artistic director.

His close association, over the years, with both the LPO and the theatre has done much to strengthen the association and raise artistic standards. It was of his period with the Orchestra that he wrote, 'there was intense competition between the London orchestras and for each other's leading players. Government support through the Arts Council, although generous for its period, had not been canalised in the form which is now a feature of the London musical scene. Grants were insufficient to give players any real security of employment. Worst of all, it was impossible for orchestras to plan ahead artistically with any "security of tenure".

'I worked for the first time with a board of directors elected by the members of the Orchestra and it was practical politics as well as personal inclination to conceal boldness of aim beneath policy of improvement in personnel and rehearsal. The day of the one-rehearsal concert, still a feature of the London scene, was slowly ending. 'In considering the merits of a player the LPO board would willingly displace one of their own directors from a leading position in the Orchestra—something which goes deeply against the grain of orchestral musicians whose life together is based on mutual trust. My task, however, was to lead, explain and to be uncompromising on essentials while making concessions on detail.

'Looking back, I feel that the board and I have little to reproach ourselves with. Gradually we improved the standard of the strings, at the same time tempting leading woodwind and brass players to join us. The first of the long annual engagements at Glyndebourne during the less busy summer months was important economically and artistically.

'In my associations with the LPO at Glyndebourne and in the concert hall, it is marvellous to sense such an atmosphere of mutual trust forged over so many years of endeavour, and to revel in the sheer enjoyment of music making.'

Before moving on to the Orchestra's activities at Glyndebourne, an association which incidentally came about in 1964, the middle period of John Pritchard's reign, it would be useful to look back momentarily at the Pritchard era, 1962–67. For it was during these years that the outline of today's Orchestra was moulded and the seeds of flair, excitement and flamboyance, were sown. The success of two major tours behind them, the Orchestra set about creating an international reputation at home. Invitations were extended to many of the world's great artists, either to make their debut or to re-appear with the Orchestra. Outstanding amongst those names in the 1960's were Eugene Svetlanov, Josef Krips, Paul Kletzki, Eugen Jochum, Maxim Shostakovich, Jascha Horenstein, Lorin Maazel and Hans Schmidt-Isserstedt.

A change in beat and environment

7

Few orchestras have a country retreat. But to the London Philharmonic Orchestra, Glyndebourne acts as just that: a welcome break in the familiar pattern of concerts, recordings and rehearsals.

It is certainly no vacation, just a change in beat and environment. For into the ten-week Glyndebourne season are crammed innumerable rehearsals and sixty performances in the atmosphere of an intimate theatre.

The over-publicised aspects of Glyndebourne—the croquet, the strawberries and cream, the evening dress in the middle of the afternoon and so on, tend to mask its intense professionalism.

Although it was not until 1964 that the LPO first played at Glyndebourne, the two came into existence, almost simultaneously. In fact it would have seemed a natural

Below left, Members of the Orchestra in stage band costume for Mozart's Don Giovanni at Glyndebourne. Right, Elisabeth Söderström

step from the outset, for until 1939 the Orchestra performed at London's best known opera venue, the Royal Opera House, Covent Garden.

The first Glyndebourne tour of Scandinavia in 1968 took in Stockholm, Oslo, Gottenburg and Copenhagen and was accompanied by the LPO in the 19-day tour. One person whose career has been closely connected with both the Orchestra and Glyndebourne is Miss Janet Baker.

'One excellent way to get to know an orchestra is to be involved in opera. After two seasons and one recording of Calisto at Glyndebourne I feel a real comradeship with the London Philharmonic Orchestra. It springs not only from sharing coffee breaks in the courtyard but from a wonderful sense of team spirit and an unmistakeable warmth coming up to the stage from the pit. There are also many lovely memories of concerts over the years and one particular moment in the recording studios, doing the Brahms Alto Rhapsody with Sir Adrian Boult, when I thought I had never heard more beautiful playing from any orchestra.'

Cartoonists, writers, comedians and critics delight in portraying conductors. The position holds mystique and power, both abused and enjoyed. It embraces the transience of a single night and the permanence of a lifetime's devotion to a passion. Above all else is the communication to a sensitive public of one particular interpretation of a score.

But occasionally there are lighter moments. One such Walter Mitty occasion was at the Royal Albert Hall in 1966 when the London Philharmonic Orchestra appeared in aid of their own national appeal fund, with Danny Kaye as their conductor.

Two fly swats, a dozen batons and a self-confessed inability to read music were his only aids. The Orchestra was stopped in full flood with a two-finger whistle; when they played too loudly he called, 'ush!'. When finally he realised that, by raising both hands during the applause at the end of a piece of music the Orchestra would stand and that by lowering his hands they would sit, it was not long before he had developed a music hall routine of another sort—with half the Orchestra leaping to its feet, whilst the other half remained seated.

Turning to the audience which included Princess Margaret, he said: 'Someone once said that an orchestra does not need a conductor. We shall find out with Ravel's Bolero.'

He gave the opening beat and then departed, flitting around the auditorium and arriving back on the rostrum just in time to conduct the final note of the final bar.

● Left, Janet Baker who in November 1971 won the Shakespeare Prize in Hamburg. Below, John Pritchard, principal conductor and artistic director 1962-1966

● The Orchestra during the final dress rehearsal of the 1971 Glyndebourne production of Macbeth

● Lighter moments at the Albert Hall in 1966 when American film artist Danny Kaye conducted the orchestra. His clowning, left, made the occasion an amusing and memorable one

● Far more regularly a guest conductor than Danny Kaye is Josef Krips, right

'To conduct gives one the greatest feeling of neurotic power' – Danny Kaye

● Left, Sir Arthur Bliss, Master of the Queen's Musick, conducting the Royal Choral Society and London Philharmonic Orchestra during an Embassy Master Series recording session at the Royal Albert Hall, 1971; one of many sessions which the Orchestra undertakes for commercial concerns from home and abroad each year. Below, Sir Arthur Bliss with the recording director John Boyden

Industrial patronage
- a helping hand

In the same year as the first of the Orchestra's national appeal concerts in 1966, a new source of income was forthcoming.

Industrial patronage of the arts is becoming increasingly important as costs outstrip guaranteed subsidies. A company which has financially helped the London Philharmonic Orchestra is W. D. & H.O. Wills.

John Wilson, their chairman and managing director, said, 'Patronage is not simply a matter of money; it is a matter also of real interest in and involvement with the Orchestra, and particularly in those areas where our commercial experience and contacts can be of real benefit to the management of the LPO and to the members of the Orchestra itself.

● **John Wilson Chairman and managing director of W D and H O Wills, whose company financially helped the Orchestra**

'In 1966 we made a grant of £5,000 to the LPO to enable them to bring to this country more of the world's finest conductors and soloists than had been possible hitherto. Since then we have continued to make an annual grant.

'Two years ago we financed two Lyrita records of the Elgar Symphonies conducted by Sir Adrian Boult; the public interest in them was such that in October, 1970 we financed the Embassy Master series on the Classics for Pleasure label which guarantees LPO six recordings a year. Within eighteen months more than a quarter of a million records had been sold and public demand is currently high.

'At the end of last year we decided to double our annual grant on the understanding that part of it would be used, at the discretion of the LPO management, for the benefit of members of the Orchestra in whatever way might seem appropriate.

'Our association has been a most rewarding one from every possible point of view, not least of which has been the pleasure it has given us to help this great Orchestra to win even greater prestige in the world of music.'

Not all performances are given with a classically-minded audience in view! Hard on the heels of the Danny Kaye success, Duke Ellington and his jazzmen combined with the LPO in 1967 to present a delightful evening's entertainment to a capacity audience at the Royal Albert Hall. This again was in aid of the Orchestra's own national appeal fund. The Duke smoothed and charmed the audience—and the LPO—in his own unmistakable style.

● An unusual combination as Duke Ellington and his jazzmen join the LPO in an evening of entertainment in 1967.

● Right, 'The

78

A thoughtful Duke Ellington discusses the score with a member of the orchestra at the Albert Hall concert.

● Members of the London
Philharmonic Orchestra in Japan
during the 1969 Far East tour

Making music in the far east

The following incident has no satisfactory conclusion. It is a story without an end. Why, therefore, is it included? Principally because it is indicative of many smaller and perhaps less memorable occasions which have happened in the careers of many orchestral players.

To Rodney Friend, leader of the Orchestra, a 10-minute recital on a violin by a youth in Manila was one of the great memories of the 1969 Far East Tour. The discovery of this prodigy, as the youth was later claimed to be, followed a request by him for Rodney Friend's autograph. He told Friend of his interest in the violin and this led to an invitation to him to play. Arriving at the appointed time, complete with a very cheap instrument, he played a Bach Prelude. Rodney Friend was absolutely staggered and moved at the wonderful music produced from such an unexpected source. As the youth came from a relatively poor family, the Orchestra management put him in touch with one of the wealthy manufacturers who had aided the Orchestra's visit, and they made arrangements for him to take up scholarship possibilities.

To others, musically, the climax of the tour was the three concerts performed in Tokyo as part of the British Trade Week.

The Orchestra's one-month, 25,000-mile, tour to Singapore, Hong Kong, the Philippines, South Korea and Japan was one of the most expensive and ambitious British artistic projects ever undertaken, and the culmination of two years of planning by the Orchestra's management. It was supported by the British Council and the Board of Trade.

In Hong Kong, the City of the Nine Dragons, with Chairman Mao's China only minutes away, there was a strangely unreal feeling in playing Berlioz and Mozart to an audience of Chinese. In Singapore, in an open-air concert in oppressive heat, the Orchestra played to an audience of 8,000 Malays and Chinese. And on their first concert night in Tokyo, the Empress of Japan made one of her rare public appearances to attend.

The whole tour was a miracle of precision and administration. A BOAC VC10 ensured the Orchestra's punctuality throughout. On one occasion, as the musicians disembarked, a pilot was heard to say rather gruffly: 'Do a good job for Britain'.

Orchestras touring abroad in fact play an ambassadorial role. Cultural exchanges, no matter in what art, bring tangible benefits as well as helping to raise world standards. Since 1962, the London Philharmonic, as a matter of policy, has endeavoured to take up every opportunity to travel overseas.

And what of the difference between British and overseas orchestras? Lord Shaftesbury, chairman of the LPO Council, had this to say during an interview:

'It may seem strange to talk of the soul of an orchestra, yet this is precisely what distinguishes the great orchestras outside this country, for instance in Berlin, Vienna, Amsterdam and Philadelphia, whether at the peak or in the trough of their artistic achievements. A lean period goes almost unnoticed by their public to whom their reputation remains unsullied.

'In London the problems are different. There are five major symphony orchestras, all in competition and all vying for the attentions of the music public. Unlike their overseas counterparts, these orchestras receive limited subsidies. A bad patch artistically or some serious miscalculation by management could spell the orchestra's end.

'Nevertheless, London is the centre of the music world and its soul the collective contribution of the five orchestras. An orchestra's identity in London depends upon the players, and theirs in turn on the orchestra's four key figures: the artistic director, the managing director, the leader and the chairman of the orchestral board. In the case of the London Philharmonic, the experience of those who occupy these positions is unsurpassed.

● **Lord Shaftesbury, chairman of the London Philharmonic Orchestra Council**

● **The LPO's first leader, Paul Beard, was followed by David McCallum, Jean Pougnet, Thomas Matthews, David Wise, Joseph Shadwick and Henry Datyner, 1957-1963 (pictured above), who was succeeded by Rodney Friend in 1964**

'The London Philharmonic Orchestra Council was formed in 1965 to support the Orchestra outside its concert and recording schedule. Its aims are to encourage the Orchestra whenever and wherever possible, as are those of the Ladies' Committee which organises so many of the appeal functions. In America the London Philharmonic Society (USA) Inc., formed prior to the 1970 visit, makes many social arrangements on the Orchestra's behalf.'

To tour extensively requires a financial stability underwritten by a multiplicity of other activities. Ever since the Orchestra's inception the word 'tour' has meant taking music outside London as well as outside Britain, but in the late 1960's it was found that the cost of travelling, and the need to preserve a strict recording schedule because of the money it brought in, had cut into the Orchestra's regional touring programme.

By 1970 there were only five centres regularly visited—Eastbourne, Hastings, Watford,

Croydon and Dorking, two of which are virtually London suburbs. However, the Orchestra is as popular in Watford now as it was in Beecham's time.

At Hastings, where they first appeared in 1947, and Eastbourne, attendances over the years have averaged 95% capacity. At the newest regional centre, the Fairfield Halls, Croydon, attendances have now reached 90% capacity.

The importance of recordings to an Orchestra's financial viability cannot be over-stressed, as Eric Bravington points out:

'Popularity, whether it be with live audiences or with those who buy our discs, is the result of every aspect of music where the Orchestra is involved. To be recognised by those who have no direct connection with music at this moment must be all to the good ultimately. This is why the advent of budget-priced records is so important. It attracts people to the Orchestra and we are in the fortunate position of having sold in excess of an unprecedented 500,000 records in 1971.'

● 'If you live in the musical culture of London, there is a danger of playing down the importance of touring abroad.' Keith Whitmore (above), Orchestra chairman and a principal horn

● Paul Beard who was leader of the orchestra on its formation in 1932

A foothold
in America

10

Since the late 1960's the Orchestra's policy has been to establish a strong foothold in America's musical activities. In 1970 the tour of New York, Philadelphia, Washington and other cities under Bernard Haitink was outstandingly successful. To consolidate their reputation the Orchestra returned to New York in 1971 and for the first time visited the west coast of America, Canada and Mexico. As most of the world's record sales are in America, the prestige of a successful tour in the USA has a direct influence upon the Orchestra's recording schedule and its cash return.

The importance of America's growing classical music public and the position of its orchestras in world music led the LPO to found the London Philharmonic Society in the USA under Lord Shaftesbury's presidency. It was this Society, coupled with the assistance of Columbia Artists and Julius Bloom, general manager of Carnegie Hall, which made the 1970-71 tours possible.

Student interest during visits to the universities particularly appealed to Eric

● **Leonard Bernstein's appearance with the London Philharmonic in the 1940s was described as 'electrifying'**

Bravington. 'The closed environment of the campus makes it possible for students to listen to and participate in making music', he says. 'The focal point of classical music in America is the university. Leonard Bernstein's presentation of classical music for the young on American television had made an enormous impact.'

Mind you, playing in the States has its highs and lows. Those on the 1971 tour remember vividly the scheduled four-hour flight from Mexico to New York. Over New York they flew in stack for two hours waiting for fog below to clear. Three abortive approaches later they flew on to Newark, but landing proved impossible there, too. On they flew to Baltimore and finally to Washington, where they touched down at 2.40 a m, ten hours after take-off. After a few hours' sleep they flew straight back to New York rather than travel by coach to make their scheduled concert appearance. Rave reviews pursued the Orchestra wherever they went. That from Harriett Johnson in the *New York Post* of October 20 was typical: ' "How can ye bloom sae fresh and fair?" we ask with Robert Burns of the London Philharmonic who settled in Carnegie Hall last night for the first of three successive concerts. Fortunately we can venture an answer judging from the rewarding impression the ensemble gave. Under the aegis of Bernard Haitink, the Philharmonic performed with exemplary discipline but extended far beyond that. Haitink has the power to inspire each of his individual choirs to play as one, yet amazingly enough each shines with a personality which belies the fact that he is dealing with groups and not individuals.'

● **Outside the Carnegie Hall following a rehearsal during the 1970 tour of the USA**

From the Albert Hall

11

In Britain, prior to the Orchestra's new world tour in 1971, one of London's musical landmarks was celebrating its centenary. The Royal Albert Hall, opened by Queen Victoria in 1871, began its second century with a Tony Bennett concert called, in contemporary idiom, 'Get happy with the LPO'.

From the thirties with Sir Thomas Beecham and Sir Henry Wood, the wartime Sunday concerts, the Promenade series and from the early fifties with their industrial concerts, the London Philharmonic has loomed large in the Royal Albert Hall's history.

The industrial series, originally designed in 1953 to attract audiences to classical music from industry and commerce, have proved so popular over the years that they have been extended to include youth groups, parties of church members, research establishments, school and college parties. Of the series, Frank Mundy, general manager of the Royal Albert Hall, while confirming their popularity, observed, 'the name "Industrial Series" gives an unfortunate impression of audiences dressed in boiler suits and cloth caps, but this is just not the case.'

One of the key figures in the Orchestra's success is its leader, Rodney Friend. His attitude is far more akin to that of the aggressively determined executive than the public's conception of an orchestral player. Here is how he presented his view of the Orchestra and his involvement with it:

'It was a challenge to accept the position of leader,' he said. 'I was 24 when I was invited by John Pritchard and the board of directors to take over. For two or three months I was probably quite ruthless—more so than I could be now, but if you want a certain standard and will not accept less, then everything and everybody within your influence has to be reviewed. After all that's partly what you have a leader for . . . it's best described as a tidying up process. If you don't cut and change in the first month, then you get to know people on a personal level which clouds your judgement.

'All orchestras have a standard level of performance—ours is high—below which you try never to sink. We all respond to conductors differently. If you are able to get with his personality then he draws out the best—if not, not. But we never sink below a standard, although it is possible for bad conductors to get acceptable performances, principally because of that level.

● The grand opening of the Royal Albert Hall of Arts and Sciences by Queen Victoria on March 29, 1871

'Between Bernard Haitink and the Orchestra the marriage is good—the entire orchestra feels good. It's a question of rapport between the leader and orchestra, and leader and conductor. Orchestras are not machines. They have good and bad periods as some musicians have poor patches—but as long as the orchestra feels there are new standards to be achieved then we will continue to progress. If we ever settled back and said we'd arrived—that would be fatal.'

At 31, in 1972, Rodney Friend was still the youngest Leader of any major London orchestra.

As I mentioned earlier, Sir Henry Wood referred to many young musicians whose careers he followed as 'my children of music.' The first of which, around whom the expression may have been coined, was Yehudi Menuhin. The youngest and certainly best known of the 'prodigies' who appeared with the Orchestra in the 1930's.

The Orchestra's policy towards young artists, conductors and composers has certainly not abated since those formative years. If anything it has strengthened and the opportunities given to those in the disciplines mentioned are more numerous. This applies both to concert performances and to recordings.

Those who have appeared are many and as yet all are not internationally recognised

90

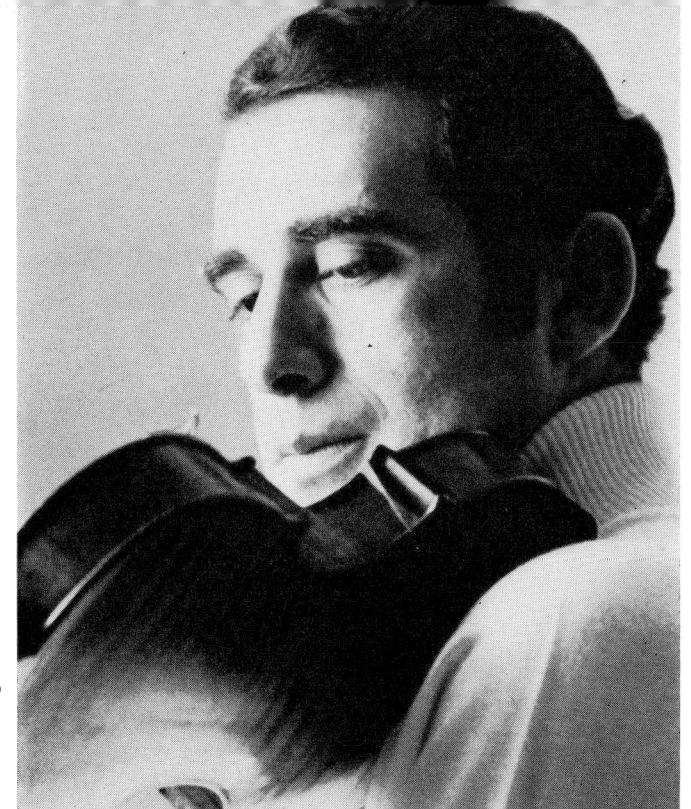

● Rodney Friend, right; whose god from age 12 to 19 was Barbirolli. 'The magnetism of his personality and the strength of the Hallé Orchestra under his direction did much for me in my early career. It was with Barbirolli that I made my first appearance at 19 in London at the Royal Festival Hall.' Below, two glum-looking violinists, Rodney Friend and Jack Benny during a concert specially arranged for television

● A capacity audience of 7000
listened enraptured to the
unusual combination of Robert
Farnon conducting the
Orchestra in a true Tony
Bennett style concert. 'This
evening has been the most
exciting and greatest episode
in all my singing career' said
Tony Bennett in 'The Stage'

92

● Daniel Barenboim, South American international concert pianist and conductor who guested with the LPO, has played with major orchestras throughout the world

● Vladimir Ashkenazy, the brilliant 35-year-old pianist from the Moscow State Conservetoire, who has played as a guest with the LPO. He is a distinguished prize-winner at international competitions at Warsaw, Belgium and Moscow

names. Some of course are, and two such names are Vladimir Ashkenazy and Daniel Barenboim. Asked about the Orchestra Vladimir Ashkenazy replied, 'I admire the London Philharmonic, not simply because of their high level of professionalism, but also because of their complete dedication to music and willingness in their everyday work. The London Philharmonic's contribution to the musical life of London is enormous and I always consider it a great honour to play with them'.

And Daniel Barenboim, 'I count my musical collaboration with the London Philharmonic Orchestra since 1959 amongst my happiest memories.'

The majority of people who meet or work with Bernard Haitink remark upon his modesty and uncomplicated approach to life. To many he is the principal reason for the Orchestra's standing in world music. At the Orchestra's offices in Welbeck Street, London, he discussed his involvement with the London Philharmonic.

'To be involved in the lives of two orchestras, one in London and the other in Amsterdam imposes a considerable strain. Yet it is so worthwhile because the contrast between the two is so stimulating. The Concertgebouw is almost fully subsidised by the Government and this has an effect upon its outlook, whereas with the London Philharmonic you are dealing with musicians who have struggled financially over

The expression is compelling, the instructions are clear as Bernard Haitink, principal conductor, rehearses the orchestra.

forty years, and won. This creates tremendous personality and a constant vibrant energy.

'With a foot in each camp—Britain and Europe—I feel that when the Common Market comes Britain will give more to Europe musically than it receives in return.

'Despite the reputation the Orchestra enjoys the players are not blasé or too polished as can be the case with other orchestras overseas. They have an air of independence. There is a good rapport between us . . . a necessary base for any lasting relationship. I would agree that London is the music capital and one reason must be the Henry Wood Promenade series. The audience here in London is certainly more aware and receptive than any other.

'My own experience with conductors is that they seem to get better with age. Their memories are like wine maturing, but the pace of music today will probably alter this. Conductors have certainly changed—the gap between them and the players is much less than it ever was.

'One of the great joys of working with the London Philharmonic is that it can be moulded to fit any occasion. I am sometimes asked which is my favourite piece of music; I have none, but if I were about to conduct the Orchestra's first concert in 1932 and wished to create an impressionable impact I would follow Sir Thomas and choose the Carnaval Romain Overture.'

We finish where we began, with the Carnaval Romain. But what of the future? The Orchestra's fortunes have changed almost with the turn of a card over the years. Now amongst the world's greatest, its artistic approach has never been more progressive or its acclaim more universal.

One final comment, from the Orchestra's chairman, Keith Whitmore:

'Bernard Haitink has said that an orchestra's best form of publicity lies in the quality of its performances. This typifies not only Haitink but also the thinking of the London Philharmonic Orchestra as a whole. There can be no doubt that Bernard Haitink's dynamic leadership, plus that rare quality of being an uncomplicated human being and a most eminent musician, plays the most important role in the Orchestra's success.'

● **Matching music to film is one of many activities which the Orchestra performs. Here the occasion, in December 1969, was recording for the Czech film 'The Battle of Neretva'. The Orchestra has also put the music to 'Lawrence of Arabia', 'Antony and Cleopatra' and many others**

The first Orchestra

12

Here is a list of Orchestral members who played at the first inaugural concert of the London Philharmonic on October 7, 1932.

First Violins
Paul Beard
B Reillie
P Frostick
B H Andrews
L Levitus
E Virgo
I Losowsky
G Whitaker
A Amery-Nichols
D Taylor
N Comras
R. Morley
A Balch
D Freedman
A G Jones
F R Drake

Second Violins
George Stratton
A Hopkinson
H Ball
W Spratt
M Sanders
L Stein
R Steel
A Kirk
H Collins
C C Draper
E Morgan
W Hulson
A Filer
L G Richards
E Roloff
H Chevreau

Violas
Frank Howard
J Dyer
W J Smith
J Cload
L Birnbaum
I Smith
W Reynolds
G M Parker
B Davis
J Denman
W Forbes
E A Christensen

Violoncellos
Anthony Pini
J Moore
C L Willoughby
J W Francis
G Marinari
G Roth
B Rickelman
T G Budd
F W Hodgkinson
D F Thomas

Double-Basses
Victor Watson
J H Silvester
S Sterling
H Green
J Hatton
C Gray
P Stanley
G Brooks
G Hatton

Flutes
Gerald Jackson
P Whitaker
J Francis

Piccolo
L Hopkinson
Oboes
Leon Goossens
H Lyons
W Whitaker

Cor Anglais
H S Green
Clarinets
Reginald Kell
L F Collins
E Flat Clarinet
E J Augarde
Bass-Clarinet
A G Stuteley

Bassoons
John Alexandra
G Holbrooke
G Vinter

Contra-Bassoon
A Alexandra

Horns
Francis Bradley
H. Burrows
T Wood
F Probyn
F Hamilton

J Phillips
J Mason
G Manners
R West

Trumpets
J H Cozens
R Dyson
R Walton
H Wild
F L Gyp

Trombones
E T Garvin
F E Stead
W H Coleman

Tenor-Tuba
H Smith

Tuba
W Scannell

Timpani
J P Bradshaw

Percussion
M E Flynn
J Hanrahan
S Beckwith
H C Weston

Harps
Marie Goossens
Muriel Cole
Julia Wolfe

The Orchestra 1972

13

Principal Conductor and Artistic Director
Bernard Haitink

Leader
Rodney Friend

President
Sir Adrian Boult

Chairman
Keith Whitmore

Managing Director
Eric Bravington

First Violins
Rodney Friend, *Leader*
Dennis Simons, *Sub-Leader*
Gerald Jarvis, *Co-Leader*

Martin Jones
David Nolan
William Leary
John Greensmith
Marie Wilson
John Kuchmy
George Apel
Michael McMenemy
Sheila Beckensall

Christine Read
Kenneth King
Vera Kantrovitch
Christopher Adey

Second Violins
John Willison, *Principal*
Robert Growcott
Geoffrey Price
Kenneth Weston
John Mayo
Brian Porter
Ronald Vaughan
Remo Lauricella
David McLaren
David Marcou
Wolfgang Kellerman
Harry Wild
Eleanor St George
Mâire Dillon

Violas
John Chambers, *Principal*
David Newland
Martin Koster
Wrayburn Glasspool
Andrew Thomas
Judith Swan
David Godsell
Frederick Buxton
Allan McDougall
Joan Wolstencroft
John G. Davis
Irmeli Rawson

'Cellos
Alexander Cameron, *Principal*
David Strange, *Co-Principal*
Santiago Carvallo
Peter Vel
John Nisbet

Ronald Calder
Thomas Francis
Michael Garbutt
David Goswell Brown

Basses
William Webster, *Principal*
Stephen Crabtree,
                    Co-Principal
Kenneth Goode
Bryan Scott
David James
George Nevison
Rodney Stewart
Geoffrey Downs

Flutes
Douglas Whittaker, *Principal*
Colin Chambers, *Co-Principal*
Robin Chapman

● **Forty years on . . . today's full orchestra with the conductor on the rostrum about to continue their role as music makers extraordinary to London and the world**